My Storytime BIBLE

Renita Boyle and Melanie Florian

Contents

God made our world 6

The good life 8

The first bad choice 10

The problem and the promise 12

The big boat 14

The big flood 16

The big rainbow 18

Longing and laughter 20

A happy romance 22

A silly swap 24

A slick trick 26

A sweet dream 28

The colourful coat 30

Prison to palace 32

Sorrow to joy 34

The basket baby 36

The burning bush 38

Red Sea rescue 40

Grumble, grump and groan 42

Loving God and living together 44

Twelve spies 46

Joshua and Jericho 48

The thankful smile 50

The listener 52

The mightiest frightiest giant 54

The kingmaker 56

The wise king 58

Just enough 60

The little hero 62

The big fish 64

Mission accomplished 66

The fiery furnace 68

Claws, jaws and silly laws 70

Good news! 72

Shepherd's delight 74

A wonderful adventure 76

Temple talk 78

Jesus is baptised 80

First followers 82

The man on the mat 84

How to pray 86

How not to worry 88

Two builders 90

The soldier's servant 92

The most important thing 94

The churning, turning lake 96

A fabulous feast 98

Waterwalkers 100

The good neighbour 102

The busy sister and the big meal 104

The good shepherd 106

Ten men well again 108

The power over death 110

The honest man's prayer 112

Jesus blesses the children 114

Blind man sees 116

The little man and the big change 118

Here comes the king 120

Dusty dirty feet 122

The special supper 124

In the garden 126

Peter denies Jesus 128

Jesus dies on a cross 130

The empty tomb 132

Thomas believes 134

Do you love me? 136

Home to heaven 138

The Holy Spirit comes to help 140

God made our world

Genesis 1:1—2:1

Before the beginning, God was there. God made everything. God spoke into the deep, dark nothing.

'Light!' he said.

There was day and night. God wrapped the world in sky and gathered the seas. There were mountains and valleys, soil and sand. Everything grew at God's command; seedlings and trees, flowers and fruit, veggies and vines. The sun began to shine. The moon and stars shimmered. Fish swam in the sea and birds sang in the air. God made every kind of animal everywhere. God was glad. It was good.

Then God made a man and a woman. Their names were Adam and Eve. God blessed them and told them to have children, enjoy the world and take care of it. God was glad. It was all very good. Then God made a special day to rest.

We are glad. God is good.

The good life

Genesis 1:26–31; 2:8–25

There were no weeds in Eden. It was a perfect garden paradise. A river flowed, fruit trees were full and the animals and birds were friendly. Adam gave them names and enjoyed their company, but he was lonely for someone like himself.

'It isn't good to be alone,' God said.

So, while Adam was asleep, God made a woman. Adam was amazed by Eve.

'She's part of me!' Adam said. God smiled because they were also a lot like him.

It was a good life tending the garden, walking and talking with God. It is good to be together with the people we love.

The first bad choice

Genesis 2:9, 15–17; 3:1–7

Everything was as it should be. The fruit from the trees, especially the one that gave life, tasted lovely and lush. But Adam and Eve never ate from the tree that had the power to let you know the difference between right and wrong.

'Don't even touch it,' God warned, 'or everything will be spoiled.' One day a sneaky serpent slipped up to Eve. 'Did God tell you not to eat fruit from any tree in the garden?'

'No,' said Eve, 'just not from the one in the middle—the one that has the power to know the difference between right and wrong—or we will die!'

'Nonsense,' said the serpent. 'God knows that you'll know what he knows.'

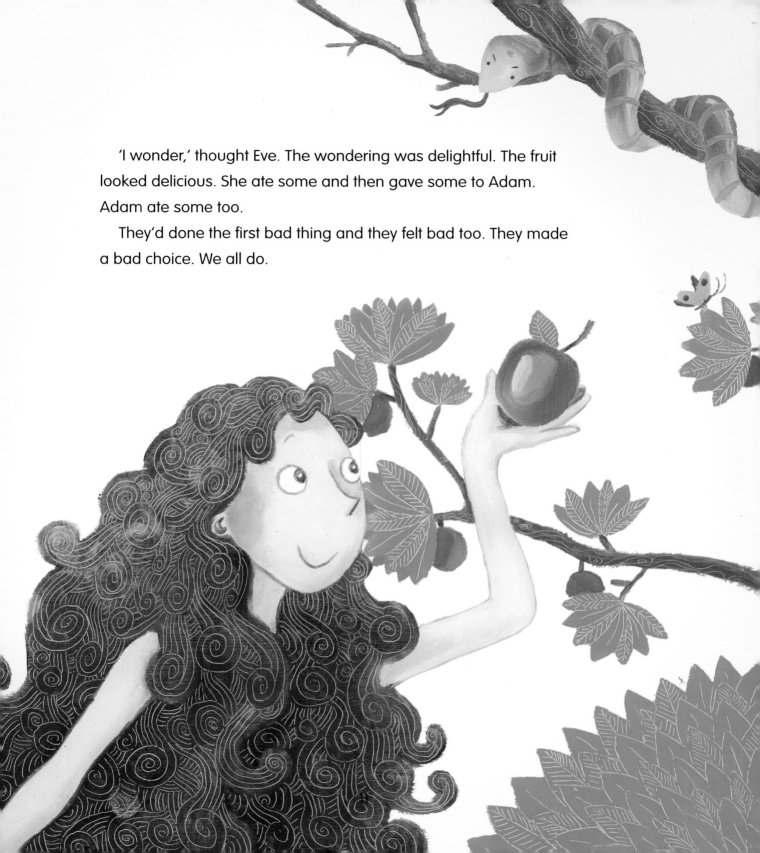

'I wonder,' thought Eve. The wondering was delightful. The fruit looked delicious. She ate some and then gave some to Adam. Adam ate some too.

They'd done the first bad thing and they felt bad too. They made a bad choice. We all do.

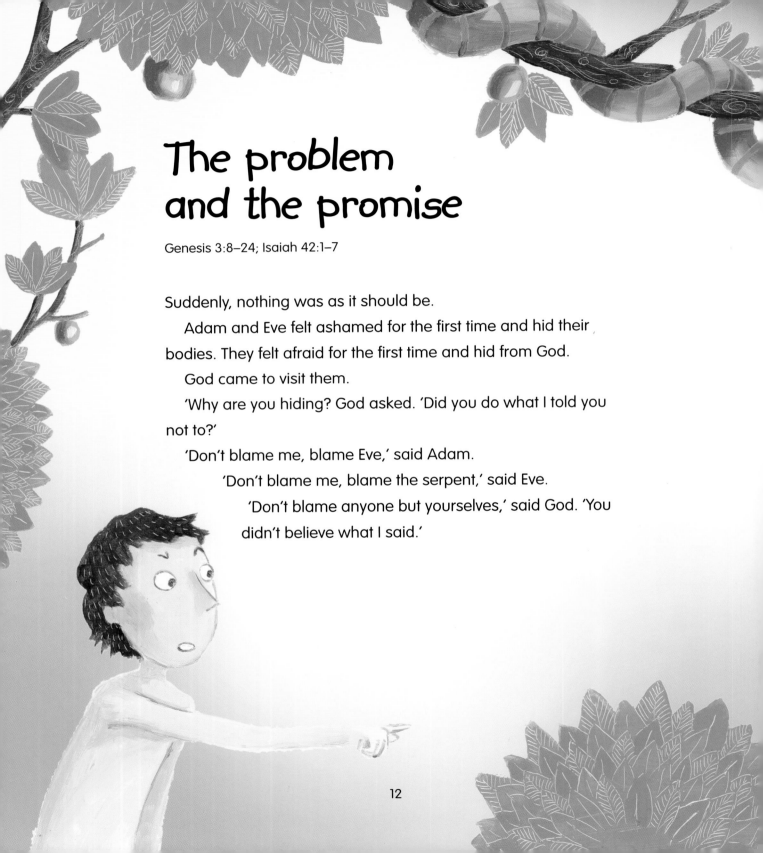

The problem and the promise

Genesis 3:8–24; Isaiah 42:1–7

Suddenly, nothing was as it should be.

Adam and Eve felt ashamed for the first time and hid their bodies. They felt afraid for the first time and hid from God.

God came to visit them.

'Why are you hiding? God asked. 'Did you do what I told you not to?'

'Don't blame me, blame Eve,' said Adam.

'Don't blame me, blame the serpent,' said Eve.

'Don't blame anyone but yourselves,' said God. 'You didn't believe what I said.'

And God knew it wouldn't be the last time.

God loved Adam and Eve, but it would be hard to stay friends. Everything would be hard. There would be thistles and thorns, pain and death. If they disobeyed him now, it would always be this way.

'You must leave my garden,' God said sadly.

God promised that he would put it right one day. A special person would come. God's enemy wouldn't be able to spoil things. Everything would once again be as it should be.

The big boat

Genesis 6:14–16, 21–22; 7:1–5

Noah lived nowhere near the sea. So everyone said it was silly
to build a big boat. Everyone also said that it was silly to believe
in God; that it was OK to forget about God and do whatever
they wanted.

Noah believed what God said instead.

'I'm going to start again,' God said sadly. 'There's
going to be a big flood. Build a boat—a big,
big boat. I'll tell you how.'

So Noah built a boat. Bang, bang,
hammer and nail. It was big
enough for himself. It was big
enough for his family. It was big
enough for two of every kind
of animal and bird and just

enough food. It was big enough to keep them safe inside. This is just where they were when the door banged shut.

When the rain began, Noah was ready.

We can be ready for anything when we believe what God says.

The big flood

Genesis 7:11–24; 8:1–12

It rained for a long time. Pit pat. It rained for a long, long time. Pit pat, pitter patter. It rained for so long that even the tippity tips of the mountain tops disappeared. Pit pat, pitter patter, swish swash swoosh. Noah's boat bobbed up and down, this way and that.

Then the rain stopped. Pit pat.

Noah waited and waited for the land to dry. Ho, hum, sigh. Then the boat bumpity bumped on the tippity top of a mountain.

Noah opened the window. It wasn't time to open the door. He watched and waited and waited some more. He sent a bird to find land. It found a place to nest.

There is a time for waiting and a time for waiting to be over.

The big rainbow

Genesis 8:15–22

Everyone was happy to get out of the boat! Birds flew free. Animals hurried and scurried. Noah's family said, 'Phew.'

Everything smelled new. A beautiful rainbow arched across the sky.

Noah thanked God for keeping them safe.

'The whole earth will never be flooded again,' God promised. 'Every rainbow will be a reminder. There will always be winter, summer, spring and harvest. Your family will grow and go everywhere on earth.'

It was a new start. We can all be thankful for new starts.

Longing and laughter

Genesis 12:1–2; 13:14–17; 15:2–6; 18:10–15; 21:1–7

Sometimes you just want to laugh. Sarah laughed when God said, 'Get ready. The baby's coming next year.'

She laughed to herself, but she laughed all the same.

It had been a long time since God promised them a baby son and more family than stars in the sky!

It had been even longer since God told them to leave home and head for a new land.

'Your family will be my special people,' God had promised. 'Someone from your family is going to bless the whole world.'

It had been longer still since they first longed for a baby.

God's promise had made them happy! They believed what God said. They did what God told them to do. But it had been a long time.

'How can we have a baby?' they laughed. 'Surely we're too old!'

'Is anything too hard for me?' asked God.

They laughed again the next year. This time everyone heard. They named their son Isaac. It means laughter.

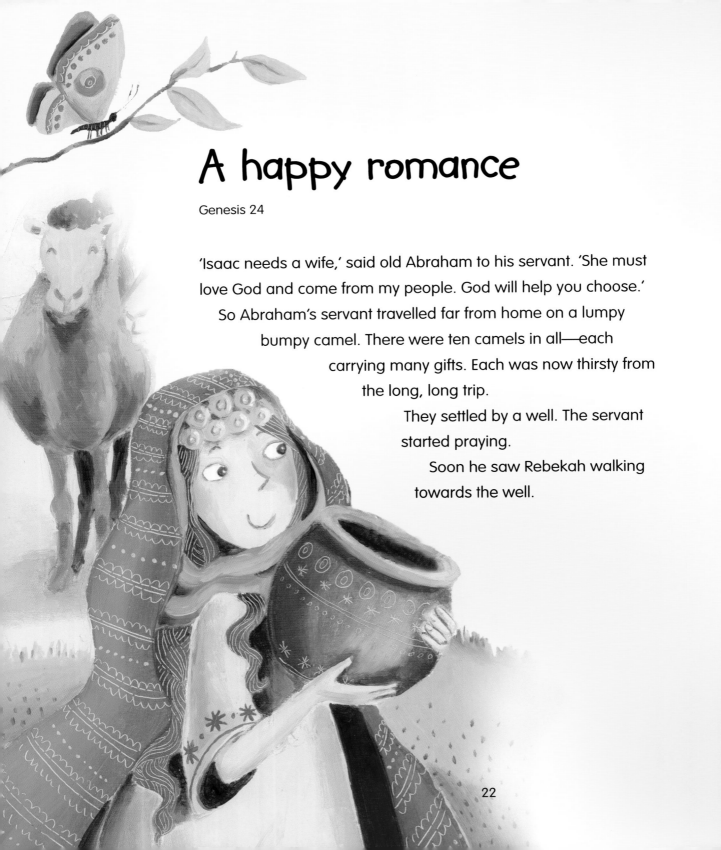

A happy romance

Genesis 24

'Isaac needs a wife,' said old Abraham to his servant. 'She must love God and come from my people. God will help you choose.'

So Abraham's servant travelled far from home on a lumpy bumpy camel. There were ten camels in all—each carrying many gifts. Each was now thirsty from the long, long trip.

They settled by a well. The servant started praying.

Soon he saw Rebekah walking towards the well.

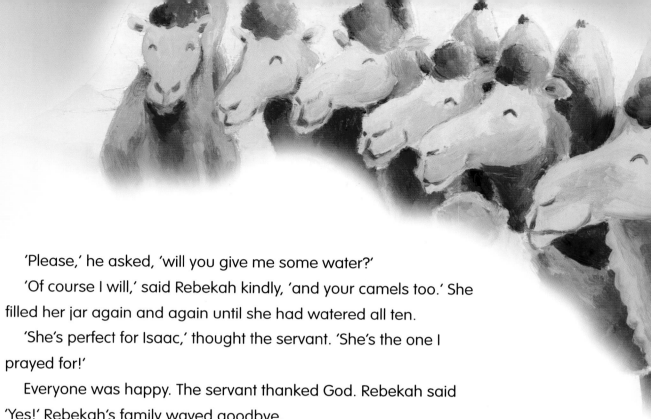

'Please,' he asked, 'will you give me some water?'

'Of course I will,' said Rebekah kindly, 'and your camels too.' She filled her jar again and again until she had watered all ten.

'She's perfect for Isaac,' thought the servant. 'She's the one I prayed for!'

Everyone was happy. The servant thanked God. Rebekah said 'Yes!' Rebekah's family waved goodbye.

Rebekah travelled far from home on a lumpy bumpy camel. Isaac was waiting for her. When Isaac met her, he was happiest of all. God's choice is always the best choice.

A silly swap

Genesis 25:19–34

All brothers argue, but Jacob and Esau fought even before they were born. They were twins, but they were not at all alike.

Esau was born first. He was strong and hairy and liked to go hunting.

Jacob was born holding on to Esau's heel. He was quiet and liked being at home with his mother, Rebekah.

One day, Esau came back from hunting with a rumbling tummy. Something yummy was simmering in Jacob's pot.

'I'm starving,' Esau grumbled. 'Give me some stew!'

Esau had no manners, but he did have something that Jacob wanted. Esau would one day be head of the family and be given God's special blessing.

'Let's swap,' said Jacob. 'You can have some stew now, if you give me your inheritance later.'

So Esau swapped his birthright for some stew and some bread.

Esau knew the stew was good. Jacob knew God's blessing is better. It always is.

A slick trick

Genesis 27:1–42

'I'm getting old and blind,' Isaac said to Esau. 'Make my favourite food. Then I will give you God's special blessing for our family.'

Rebekah overheard every word. While Esau went hunting, Rebekah started scheming.

'Hurry, Jacob!' she said. 'I'll cook for your father. You pretend to be your brother.'

'But Mother,' Jacob said, 'Father will know! Esau is hairy!'

'Just do as I say, son,' she said.

So Jacob dressed in Esau's clothes. He covered his arms in goat hair and took the food to his father. It would be a slick trick.

'I'm back!' Jacob said, pretending to be Esau.

'That was quick,' said Isaac.

'God helped me,' Jacob lied.

'Come closer,' Isaac replied. 'You sound like Jacob, but you do feel like Esau.'

Isaac promised Jacob God's blessing. There was nothing left for Esau.

Jacob had fooled his father and cheated his brother. He also had to leave his mother.

'When Father dies,' Esau raged, 'I will kill my brother.'

Some tricks are not so slick.

27

A sweet dream

Genesis 28:10–22

Jacob ran away from Esau but he couldn't run away from what he had done. He worried as he went. He wanted to go home. That night, he slept with his head on a rock—and Jacob dreamed. He saw the angels that are always around us but seldom seen. Then he saw God!

'I was with your grandfather, and your father too,' said God. 'I promise to protect you and always be with you. This land will be yours. Your family will be bigger than you can imagine. Someone special will come from your people and bless the whole world.'

Jacob woke up amazed and thought, 'I met God on this spot!'

He tipped the rock upright and left it there so that he would always remember God's special care.

'I will make you my God too,' promised Jacob. 'If you keep your promise, I will follow you.'

The colourful coat

Genesis 37

Joseph loved his colourful coat. He was Jacob's favourite son and he knew it. His eleven brothers knew it too! They were green with envy. They hated Joseph's coat. They hated Joseph's dreams. They hated… Joseph.

'In my dreams you all bow down to me!' Joseph said.

His brothers had had enough. 'We'll never bow to you,' they huffed.

One day, they were working in the field. Joseph was coming. They were so angry they saw red.

'Let's kill him,' they said.

'Let's not,' said Reuben. 'We can throw him in this black pit instead.'

So they grabbed Joseph, took his coat and did just that.

As they were having lunch, some traders came by on the way to Egypt. Their camels were loaded with things to sell.

Judah had an idea. 'They can sell Joseph as well!'

So they sold their brother for 20 silver coins. They killed a goat and covered the coat with blood. Jacob thought Joseph was dead. He was heartbroken.

Joseph felt blue too. He would soon be far away from everything he knew.

Prison to palace

Genesis 39—41

Joseph was in jail but he trusted God. He knew God had a plan. One day the king of Egypt asked to see Joseph.

'I've been having strange dreams,' said the king. 'Can you tell me what they mean?'

'God will tell me and I will tell you,' said Joseph. 'Then you'll know just what to do.'

Joseph listened to the king. The king told Joseph everything.

'There were seven fat cows grazing by the river. Then seven skinny cows ate them for dinner!'

God helped Joseph to understand.

'For seven years there will be lots of food for everyone. Then there will be seven years when there is none. You need a plan!'

'Joseph, I have a job for you,' said the king. 'You can tell us what to do!'

So Joseph got to work. While the crops were good, Joseph stored up extra food. When the crops went bad, Joseph shared out what they had. Joseph was in charge of everything and was treated almost like a king!

Sorrow to joy

Genesis 42—45

When the bad years came, people travelled to Egypt from far away. Joseph's big brothers came to see him one day.

It had been a long time. Joseph looked like a king! Joseph knew his brothers, but they did not know him!

They bowed down on their knees.

'We have come to buy some food,' they said. 'Can you help us, please?'

Joseph was amazed at this sight. He remembered his dreams. His dreams were right!

Joseph stored up lots of food, but in his heart he stored up good.

He gave his brothers grain to fill their sacks. When they needed more, they came back. Their youngest brother Benjamin was with them too. Joseph was so happy! He just had to tell.

'It's me—your brother Joseph! I am alive and well!'

His brothers were so sorry for what they'd done.

'You hurt me. It is true,' said Joseph. 'But God used it for good. Now I can help you! I choose to forgive. Bring Father with you and come here to live!'

The basket baby

Exodus 1:22—2:10

The new king of Egypt hated God's people living in his land.
He was very cruel.

36

'Throw all their baby boys in the river Nile!' said the nasty king with a nasty smile.

Jochabed had a sweet little son. She sang a sweet song all night long.

'Hush little baby. Don't say a thing. We must keep you a secret from the nasty king.'

But the baby got bigger as babies always do. Now what was his sweet mother to do? She made a basket and tucked him safe inside. Then she hid the basket by the riverside. Big sister Miriam kept watch close by.

Now a pretty princess with a pretty smile often took a bath in the river Nile. She saw the basket bobbing and the baby tucked inside.

'Hush little baby. Don't you cry,' she sighed. 'I will love you. I will not let you die!'

Miriam saw how the princess loved her brother.

'I know someone who can help to look after him!' said Miriam. Then she went to get their mother.

Jochabed held her sweet little son and sang a sweet song all night long.

'Hush little Moses. God knows everything. You are now a prince in the palace of a king!'

The burning bush

Exodus 3—12

Moses hated how the king treated God's people. All day, every day, they were forced to work hard. All day, every day, they cried out to God.

One day, Moses saw something amazing. A bush was blazing but it didn't burn up.

God spoke to Moses.

'I am going to save my people. Tell the king to set them free!'

Moses was afraid, but he did as he was told. He went to the king and said, 'Let God's people go!'

38

'No!' said the king. 'They belong to me! They don't belong to your God. I will not set them free!'

Then all day, every day, he worked them even more. All day, every day, harder than before.

So Moses went to warn the king.

'Let God's people go! There will be trouble if you continue to say no!'

The river ran red. There were frogs, flies and bugs. Animals died and people got sores. There was hail, fire and darkness. Locusts ate the crops the people sowed. But the king's heart grew even harder. He would not let God's people go.

Finally, the king's eldest son was among many sons who died.

'Take your people, Moses. Go from here!' the king cried.

Red Sea rescue

Exodus 14:1—15:21

It didn't take long for God's people to pack. And it didn't take long for the king to want them back.

'After them!' he shouted. 'Don't let them get away!'

Then all the king's horses and all the king's men chased after God's people. The king led the way.

They were almost to the sea. The soldiers were near. There was nowhere to go! They were trapped and full of fear!

'We could have stayed where we were and died!' they cried. 'Why did you bring us here?'

But it was God who had rescued them; God would set them free.

Moses raised his stick—and a path opened through the sea!

The soldiers tried to follow, but the waves came crashing down. God's people were safe on the other side. None of them was drowned.

They sang their thanks to God and cheered and danced around. The praise of God's people is such a joyful sound!

Grumble, grump and groan

Exodus 16:1–16; 17:1–7; 40:34–38

They were going to a new land. God promised it would be their own.
But all they seemed to do was mumble, mump and moan.

'We're hungry! We're tired! We're thirsty!' they whined. 'We
should have stayed at home.'

'God takes care of us every day,' said Moses. 'How quickly
you forget. We have manna, meat and water. There is no
need to fret!'

God saved them from slavery. God never left them alone.
But all they seemed to do was grumble, grump and groan.

'How long until we get there?' they muttered. 'We just want
to go back home.'

'God shows us the way every day,' said Moses. 'How quickly
you forget. God is in the cloud and fire ahead of us. There is no
need to fret!'

God was patient with his people everywhere they roamed. God
is patient with us too, even when we grumble, grump and groan.

42

Loving God and living together

Exodus 19—20; Mark 12:30–31

God gathered his people by a big mountain. Thunder clapped. Lightning crashed. A thick cloud covered the mountain. The people quivered. Moses went up to meet with God.

'I promise to make you my people,' God said. 'But you must promise to do what I say.'

The people promised, but it wasn't going to be easy. They didn't know how to love God and live God's way. So God spoke from the smoke.

'I am God. I saved you and love you very much.

Never worship idols you can see or touch.

I am the only God. You must worship only me.

When you say my name, say it lovingly.

There are six days for working and a seventh day for rest. Remember to remember me and you will be blessed.

Respect your parents.

Do not murder.

Be true to your husband or wife.

Do not take what isn't yours.

Don't be jealous and don't tell lies.'

These ten rules—the Ten Commandments—give us all a clue. God loves us. We must love God too! Treat other people as you want them to treat you.

Twelve spies

Numbers 13—14; Deuteronomy 1

They were almost to the Promised Land. Moses was excited, but the people didn't know what to expect.

'We're here! Let's go and win it,' said Moses.

'We're not so sure! Let's see what's in it,' said the people.

So Moses picked twelve men to take a look and come back again.

As the people set up camp, the spies set out to find out everything they could.

Caleb and Joshua came back carrying a huge and heavy cluster of grapes.

'God keeps his promises,' they said. 'It is a good land!'

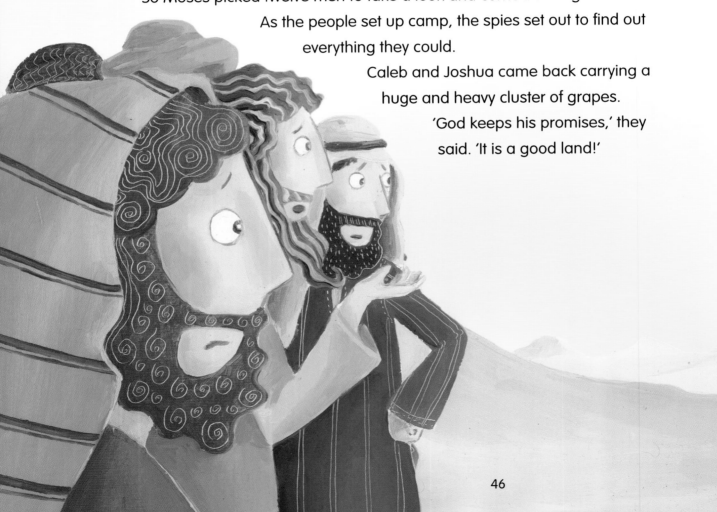

'On the other hand,' said the other spies, 'the people are huge and we are small. The cities have walls that are heavy and tall.'

'God is with us!' said Caleb and Joshua. 'Let's go and get it!'

'We're afraid,' God's people cried. 'Can't we just forget it?'

God saw what was happening. He saw that his people still didn't trust him.

'After everything you've seen me do,' he said, 'you still don't think I'll take care of you. You are not ready to live in the Promised Land.'

By the time they were, they had wandered in the desert for 40 years. It's better to trust God than give in to our fears.

Joshua and Jericho

Joshua 6:1–20

When Moses died, Joshua became the leader of God's people. He believed what God said. The people did too. This time they would be ready to enter the Promised Land.

'This is the plan,' God told Joshua. 'I want you to go to Jericho. The gate is shut tight, the walls are strong. But, if you do what I say, the walls will fall down. The walls will all fall down.'

So they marched around the town, round and round the town. Once a day for six days they marched without a sound—no one said a word. Only their trumpets could be heard. The people inside Jericho thought it quite absurd.

On the seventh day Joshua and his men marched seven times round and round the town. The trumpets blew! The men gave a shout! Those walls came tumbling down and down. The walls came tumbling down!

The thankful smile

Ruth 1—4

Naomi's husband and two sons had died. She looked at her daughters-in-law one day.

'I am old,' she said. 'I can do nothing for you. You should go back to your own families.'

Orpah was sad, but she went on her way.

Ruth said, 'I will not leave you all alone. I will go with you—your God will be my own.'

Naomi smiled a thankful smile.

They went to live in Bethlehem where Naomi had lived as a child. They were poor and hungry there.

'I am old,' Naomi said to Ruth. 'I can do nothing for you.'

But Ruth said, 'I will care for you. I will gather grain. Trust God. Life will be good again.'

Naomi smiled a thankful smile.

Boaz owned the fields. He saw Ruth working hard every day.

'She takes care of Naomi and is very kind,' said a worker. 'She gathers the grain we leave behind.'

'Naomi must love her very much,' Boaz said.

Then Boaz began to love Ruth too.

Naomi smiled a thankful smile.

Boaz and Ruth became husband and wife. They cared for Naomi for the rest of her life. She did trust God and life was good again. When Boaz and Ruth had a baby son, Naomi smiled a thankful smile.

The listener

1 Samuel 3

Young Samuel lived in God's house with old Eli, the priest. He was learning how to serve God.

It had been a busy day. Samuel was a sleepy boy. He went to bed and closed his eyes. He heard someone calling.

'Samuel.'

He rose and ran to Eli.

'Here I am,' said Samuel.

'I didn't call you,' Eli said. 'Go back to bed, sleepy head.'

Samuel closed his eyes. Then he heard his name again.

He rose and ran to Eli.

'I'm here,' said Samuel.

'I didn't call,' Eli said. 'Go back to bed.'

Samuel closed his sleepy eyes. A third time someone called.

Samuel rose and ran to Eli.

'Here I am,' he said.

'God is calling you,' said wise old Eli. 'Next time, tell him you're listening.'

Samuel went off to bed. Soon he heard God calling again.

'Samuel! Samuel!'

'I'm listening,' Samuel said.

God often spoke to Samuel and Samuel grew wise. Samuel never stopped listening to God. We are all wise when we listen.

The mightiest frightiest giant

1 Samuel 17:1–50

Goliath was the mightiest frightiest giant God's army had ever seen. He wore giant armour and held a giant sword. He also had a giant voice.

Every day he shouted, 'I'm the biggest giant you ever did see. None of you is brave enough to come and fight me.'

And because no one was, God's enemies were winning.

Now David was the youngest and the smallest of his brothers. He was also the bravest. One day, he heard Goliath boasting.

'I'm not afraid,' David said. 'I'll fight that big bully.'

'You're too small,' said King Saul. 'At least put on some armour!'

But David chose his shepherd's sling.

'You can't beat Goliath with that thing,' said the king.

'I can't,' David said, 'but God can!'

And off he went to fetch five stones and face Goliath. It only took one. It hit Goliath on the head and the giant fell down dead.

God's army cheered. God's enemies ran away. God is the mightiest and the greatest.

The Kingmaker

1 Samuel 8—10; 15:1—16:13

Samuel helped the people listen to God, but they wanted a king instead.

'Everyone else has a king,' they said.

'We're not like everyone else,' said Samuel. 'God is our king.'

Samuel spoke to God. God was sad too. 'They are rejecting me; they are not rejecting you.'

God helped Samuel choose a king, even though he knew the trouble it would bring. King Saul was handsome and tall.

'Long live the king!' the people cheered.

'Love God and obey him!' Samuel warned.

When King Saul wouldn't obey God, God helped Samuel choose someone who would.

'He will be one of Jesse's sons,' said God.

Samuel thought God would choose the oldest. He was tall like Saul.

'No,' said God. 'He's not the one at all.'

God chose David, the very youngest, instead. He took care of sheep, played the harp and loved God with all his heart.

'One day David will be king. He loves me more than anything,' God said.

God knows good looks aren't everything.

The wise King

1 Kings 3:5–15; 8:54–66; 10:1–29

When Solomon became king, God said, 'Ask me for anything.'

'Anything?' asked the king.

'Anything,' answered God.

Solomon liked gold. He liked to win battles. He liked the idea of living a long life. But he loved God. He wanted to be a good ruler and make good choices.

'I don't know anything about being a king,' said Solomon. 'So what I'd like best of all is to be wise.'

God liked Solomon's answer.

'You will have wisdom,' God said, 'and fortune and fame! Everyone will know your name!'

And so they did! Even the Queen of Sheba who lived far, far away!

Solomon made good choices, gave good advice and he made a grand temple for God's people to worship in. They had a grand festival to celebrate.

'God is good!' Solomon said. 'God keeps his promises!'

Solomon was wise to praise God's name. We can be wise and do the same.

Just enough

1 Kings 17:8–16

There was too much sun and not enough rain. There was not enough grain to make bread. There was not enough water to drink.

God sent Elijah to a woman for help. She was out gathering firewood when he came. They were both hungry and thirsty.

'May I have some water and bread?' asked Elijah.

'I have just enough flour and oil to make bread for one last meal,' she said. 'Then my son and I will die.'

'God will take care of you,' said Elijah.

So the kind woman gave Elijah some water and baked him some bread. The jar of flour should have been empty, but it wasn't. The jug of oil should have been empty, but it wasn't.

From that day on until there was just enough rain, she had just enough flour and oil over and over again.

The little hero

2 Kings 5:1–16

Everyone tried to be kind, but General Naaman knew they were looking at him. His skin was blotchy, and itchy too. There was nothing any doctor could do..

'I know someone who can help!' said the girl who served his wife. 'Elisha will ask God to heal General Naaman and it will change his life.'

So Naaman saddled up his horse and went to Elisha's house.

Naaman was a hero. But he felt like a nobody when Elisha didn't even come to meet him. Elisha sent a messenger instead.

'Wash seven times in that river and you will be well,' he said.

Naaman was annoyed. 'What does this mean? Why wash in a river that isn't even clean?'

'If you believe what God says,' said Naaman's servant, 'maybe you can be clean.'

So Naaman washed seven times. When he was done, his skin was as good as new!

He ran to Elisha and said, 'I know your God is true!'

He thanked Elisha and tried to pay him in gold.

'No,' said Elisha. 'God is the real hero.'

And so was the little servant girl, if the truth be told.

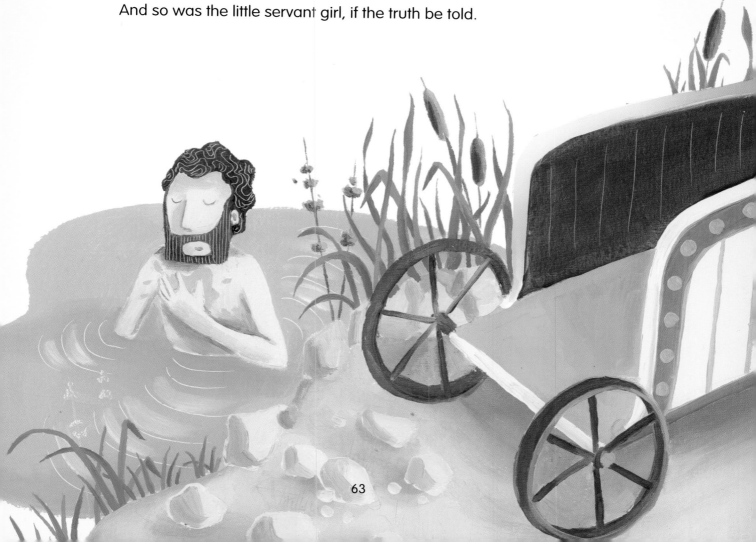

The big fish

Jonah 1—2

'Jonah, go to Nineveh,' God said. 'Tell the people I see the bad things they are doing. I want them to change.'

God said, 'Go!' but Jonah said, 'No!' He was afraid and jumped on a ship sailing far away.

While Jonah slept, a storm stirred. Thunder crashed. Lightning flashed. The sailors were scared.

'We're going to sink,' they screamed.

The captain shook Jonah. 'Wake up! Do something! Pray!'

'It's my fault,' said Jonah. 'I'm running away from God. Throw me into the sea and you will be safe.'

So they did.

The storm stopped. The sailors were saved. So was Jonah.

Glub, gulp, swish, swish. Jonah was swallowed by a great big fish! He had time to think. He had time to thank God and pray.

'I'm truly sorry for running away,' he told God. 'I will keep my promise to do whatever you ask.'

The big fish burped. Jonah bounced on to a beach. Jonah got a second chance.

It's best to say yes the first time.

Mission accomplished

Jonah 3—4

Jonah liked telling the people of Nineveh that God was cross with them. He thought they should get into trouble.

'God says to change your wicked ways or else!' Jonah said.

He never thought they would. But they did! They were truly sorry and showed it. They asked God to forgive them and help them.

God gave them a second chance too.

Jonah was cross. 'I knew you would forgive them,' he sulked. 'It's so unfair after all the bad things they have done.'

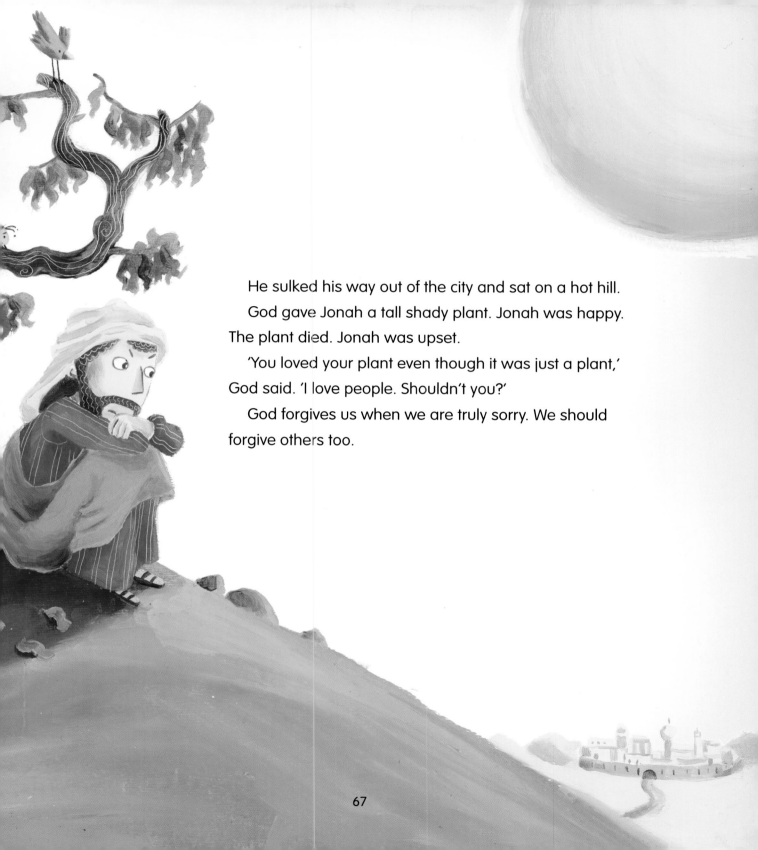

He sulked his way out of the city and sat on a hot hill.

God gave Jonah a tall shady plant. Jonah was happy. The plant died. Jonah was upset.

'You loved your plant even though it was just a plant,' God said. 'I love people. Shouldn't you?'

God forgives us when we are truly sorry. We should forgive others too.

The fiery furnace

Daniel 3

King Nebuchadnezzar made a huge golden statue. He told everyone to bow down and worship it or be thrown into a flaming furnace.

Shadrach, Meshach and Abednego said, 'No!'

'Bow down,' fumed the king, 'or into the fire you'll go!'

They would not do what they were told.

'You are great,' they said, 'but God is greater still! If God wants to save us, we know he will. We will worship God alone, not a statue made of gold!'

The furnace raged, the king raged hotter. He turned up the heat seven times higher! The men were tied up and tossed into the fire. The king gazed into the blaze. He was amazed.

'There are four men,' he said, 'not three! One is an angel. Quick, set them free!'

Shadrach, Meshach and Abednego were unhurt, unafraid, unsinged and untied.

'You don't even smell of smoke!' the king cried.

He told everyone that God alone could save.

'A king is great, but God is greater still. God will save us.'

We know he will.

Claws, jaws and silly laws

Daniel 6

Daniel lived far from home but he was close to God. Day in, day out, three times a day, Daniel knelt by his window to pray.

King Darius knew that Daniel was wise and honest. He trusted Daniel's good advice. This made the king's other advisers jealous. They knew that Daniel was a praying man, so they devised a nasty plan.

'King, live for ever!' they said. 'Here's what to do. Everyone should pray only to you! Anyone who doesn't should be arrested and then thrown into the lions' den!'

The king liked this law a lot. He forgot about Daniel—but his advisers did not.

Day in, day out, especially that day, Daniel got down on his knees to pray. He asked God to be near him and then... Daniel was thrown into the lions' den.

The king couldn't sleep that night. He ran to the den in the morning light.

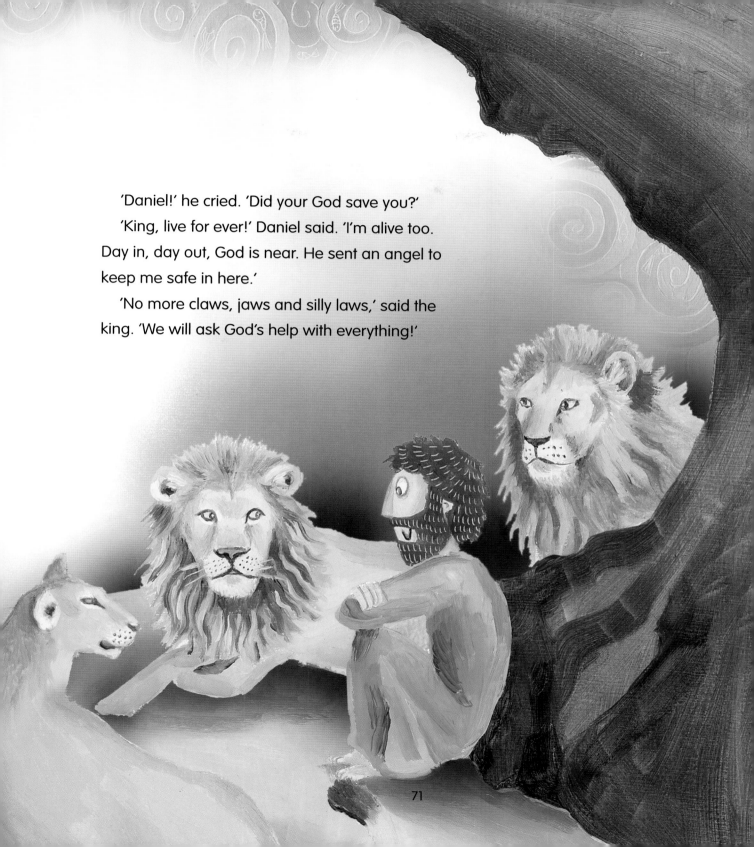

'Daniel!' he cried. 'Did your God save you?'

'King, live for ever!' Daniel said. 'I'm alive too. Day in, day out, God is near. He sent an angel to keep me safe in here.'

'No more claws, jaws and silly laws,' said the king. 'We will ask God's help with everything!'

Good news!

Matthew 1:18–25; Luke 1:26–38; 2:1–7

An angel came to see Mary. She was afraid.

'Don't worry,' said the angel. 'God has chosen you! There is nothing God can't do. You will be the mother of God's own son. He will show people how to live for God and forgive the wrong they've done. People here, people there, all kinds of people everywhere!'

When an angel came to see Joseph, he was afraid.

'Don't worry,' said the angel. 'God has chosen you, too! You will marry Mary and help her to raise God's son. He will show people how to live for God and forgive the wrong they've done. People here, people there, all kinds of people everywhere!'

When it was almost time for the baby to be born, Mary and Joseph travelled to Bethlehem. They tried to find a place to stay, but all the inns were full that day! People here, people there, all kinds of people everywhere!

'Don't worry,' said an innkeeper. 'You can stay in my barn.'

So Mary and Joseph did their best to settle down and have a rest. It wasn't long until the time came! Mary had a baby son. They named him Jesus. It means 'God saves'. People here, people there, all kinds of people everywhere!

Shepherd's delight

Luke 2:8–20

It was quiet on the hill that night. Some shepherds were watching their sheep nearby. Suddenly they saw a dazzling light.

'Don't be afraid,' an angel said. 'I bring you good news with great delight! A baby was born this very day and is lying in a bed of hay. He is the one God sent to save.'

Before the shepherds could think what to do, many other angels gathered there too. They all praised God and began to sing, 'Glory to the newborn king! Peace on earth for everyone!'

Then as quickly as they came, the angels were gone. The shepherds stood there all alone. They looked at each other, they looked at their sheep. They knew they'd never get to sleep.

The shepherds were filled with such delight, they ran to town that starry night! They found the baby where the angel had said, snuggled up warm in a manger bed: the one God sent to save.

They smiled at the baby fast asleep. Then they went back to the hill to take care of their sheep. They sang praises to God all through the night and spread the good news with great delight.

75

A wonderful adventure

Matthew 2:1–12

'There's a new star!' said the wise men. 'Where's the new king?'

And off they went on a wonderful adventure. They followed the star far away, wondering as they went. When they got to King Herod's palace they wondered out loud.

'Where's the newborn king?' they asked. 'We saw his star from afar and want to worship him!'

When King Herod heard, he was most upset.

'I don't want to be the old king yet!' he stomped.

'God promised a special new king,' his advisers said. 'Everyone is waiting for him. He will be born in Bethlehem.'

King Herod had a nasty plan to kill the new king. He called the wise men.

'When you find him,' he said sweetly, 'you must tell me too so I can worship him just like you!'

When they did find Jesus, their smiles were as bright as the star. They knelt down and gave him gifts: gold, frankincense and myrrh.

King Herod waited, but the wise men did not go back. God sent them a new way home, wondering about the new king as they went.

Temple talk

Luke 2:41–52

Jesus wasn't lost. Not really. He knew exactly where he was. But Mary and Joseph didn't. They were lost in worry. The streets were crowded and they had been looking frantically, asking everyone, shouting everywhere for three days. They couldn't sleep. They couldn't eat. They couldn't think of anything else.

Finally, they found him. He was talking with the teachers in the temple. He was lost in his thoughts about God. The teachers were amazed at how wise he was for a twelve-year-old. Mary and Joseph were amazed too.

'Jesus!' Mary cried. 'Where have you been? We have been looking everywhere for you!'

Tears filled her eyes. Jesus looked surprised.

'I didn't mean to worry you,' he said. 'I've been here in my Father's house. I thought you knew.'

'We're just so glad to see you, son!' they said, hugging him.

'I'm glad to see you too,' Jesus said. Then they all went home.

Jesus obeyed Mary and Joseph as he had always done. He also pleased God and grew up wise and strong.

Jesus is baptised

Matthew 3:13–17; Mark 1:9–11; Luke 3:1–20

John was preaching loud and clear.

'God's promised one will soon be here! Love God! Live God's way! God's kingdom is near!'

People were sorry for the wrong they had done. They wanted to know that God had forgiven them. John wanted to show it by baptising them in the river.

'This is only water,' he said. 'The one who is coming will wash you with the Holy Spirit instead!'

Then one day, Jesus came to be baptised. John knew he was the one!

'It's me that needs to be washed by you!' said John.

But Jesus said, 'Let's do what pleases God.'

When Jesus came out of the water, the heavens opened. The Holy Spirit settled on him as gently as a dove.

'I love my son so much,' said a voice. 'I am happy with everything he does.'

First followers

Matthew 4:18–22; Mark 1:16–20; Luke 5:1–11

It was morning. Peter and Andrew, James and John had been fishing all night, and not got a nibble. Now they were washing their nets.

There was a crowd on the beach listening to Jesus teach.

'Everyone can be part of God's kingdom,' he said.

The crowd got bigger and bigger. Jesus got into Peter's boat and they bobbed away from shore.

'God loves you! Love God too! Live God's way and love others the way that God loves you!'

When Jesus was finished, he turned to Peter and said, 'I feel like fishing!'

'I've already been,' said Peter. 'Not a nibble.'

'Let's try again!' said Jesus. So they did.

Suddenly, there were more fish than a fisherman could wish for. The nets were bursting!

'Come and help!' shouted Peter to the others.

Soon both boats were so full they began to sink! Peter began to think. He fell to his knees and said, 'Lord, I've done so many wrong things!'

'Come on,' Jesus said to them. 'Follow me and we'll fish for people until God's kingdom is bursting!' And they did.

The man on the mat

Matthew 9:1–8; Mark 2:1–12; Luke 5:17–26

Jesus was teaching. The house was packed. People could hardly move..

The man on the mat couldn't move at all. But he had four friends who carried him where he needed to go.

'Let's go and see Jesus,' they said. 'He can help you!'

'How can we do that?' said the man. 'No more people can get through the door.'

The friends had a chat.

'Who needs a door? The roof is flat! We'll knock a hole through and lower you.'

'Good plan,' said the man.

'Where there's a will, there's a way,' said his friends.

The four friends carried the man on his mat. They climbed on to the roof that was flat. They knocked a hole through and lowered their friend down to Jesus.

Jesus looked at the man in amazement. Then he looked up at the friends and smiled. He saw faith in their eyes and hope on their faces.

'All will be well,' he said. 'Your sins are forgiven,' he said to the man, 'and you can walk!'

The man carried his own mat. He jumped, skipped and walked by himself. And that was the beginning of that!

How to pray

Matthew 6:7–14; Luke 11:1–4

Jesus' friends wanted to know how to pray. Jesus showed them what to do.

'Keep it simple. Use your own words. Mean what you say. God knows how you are feeling even before you pray.

'Talk to God as a loving Father who wants what is best for you. You are God's child. God wants to be with you.

'Remember God's name is holy and what God says is true.

'Ask God to be the king of everything. Pray that God will help you do what he wants you to.

'Pray for the things you need to live.

'Ask him to forgive you and to help you to forgive.

'Pray that God will keep you safe, and help you choose to live his way.'

How not to worry

Matthew 6:19–21, 25–34; 7:7–12

Jesus was teaching on a hillside. It was a lovely day. The birds were singing. The flowers were blooming. But people were worrying as people often do.

'Don't worry about what you will eat or drink or wear,' said Jesus. 'Just look at the birds in the air. They don't sow seeds for food to eat. God takes care of all their needs.

'Will worrying make you stronger or help you live longer?

'See the flowers that grow? They don't sew their own clothes, but they are more beautiful than King Solomon's robes.

'God loves you even more than the birds and the flowers.

'There's more to life than fashion and food. God will take care of you.

God is good.

'If you look for something, you find it. If you knock on a door, someone answers it. If you ask your parents for bread, do they give you a stone instead? Ask God for the things you need and you will receive. God is good. Do you believe?

'Don't put your trust in the things that you own. Things are easily lost or stolen or worn. God's treasures last for ever. Gather these and you will have all that you need.

'Worry doesn't change a thing. Trust God for everything.'

Two builders

Matthew 7:24–27; Luke 6:47–49

Many people who listened to Jesus promised to live God's way. But not all of them kept their promises. Jesus told them this story.

'There were once two builders. Each of them wanted to build a house. The first builder was wise. His plan was sound. He chose to build on solid ground. He dug down deep and laid a firm foundation. The work was hard and long but the house he built was sturdy and strong. When the rain lashed down and the floods flashed up, the house on the rock withstood the storm. Those who do what I say, and live God's way, are like this.

'The second builder was foolish. He had
no plan. He chose to build on sandy land.
The house looked grand and went up fast.
But when the rain lashed down and the flood
flashed up, the house didn't last. It crashed!
Those who promise to do what I say, but
don't, are like this.

'Don't call me your Lord unless you mean
what you say,' said Jesus. 'Those who follow
me must live God's way.'

91

The soldier's servant

Matthew 8:5–13; Luke 7:1–10

One day, an officer from the Roman army rushed up to Jesus.

'Please help!' he begged. 'My servant is in pain and can't move his legs! I know that you have the power to heal.'

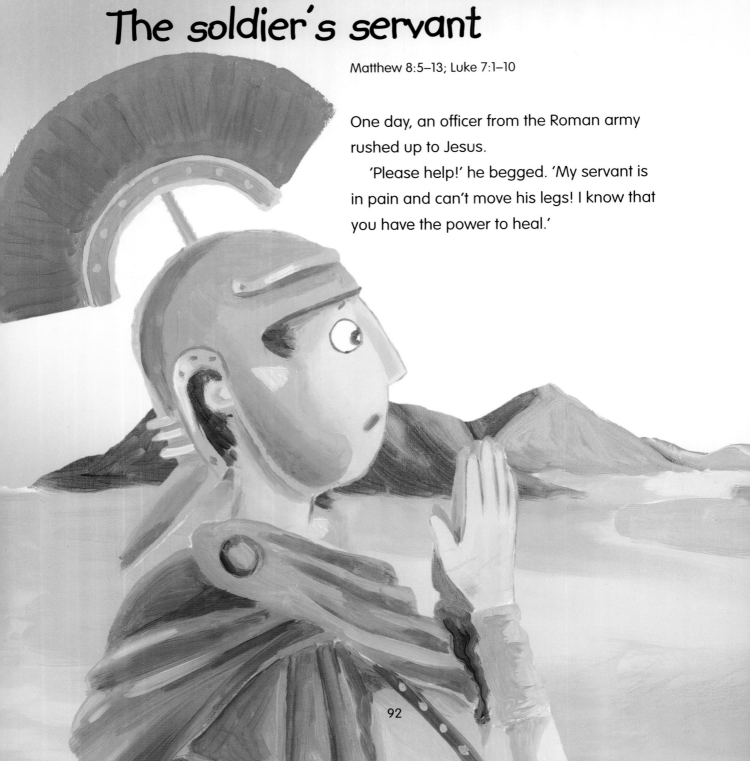

Jesus could see that his faith was real.

'I will come right now and make your servant well.'

'You don't need to come,' the officer said. 'You can make him better from just where you are. I tell my soldiers what to do and they obey. You can command illness to go away. Just say the word.'

Jesus was amazed by what he heard.

'I have never found so much faith in anyone! Not even in Israel! Go home. Your servant will be well.'

And he was.

The most important thing

Matthew 13:44–46; Mark 12:28–34

Jesus travelled from town to town. He showed people how to love God and live God's way. One day, a man was listening..

'What is the most important thing God wants us to do?' the man asked.

'God loves you completely. Love God completely too!' Jesus answered. 'And treat other people as you want them to treat you.'

'I understand,' said the man. 'I should give myself to God before I give him any other thing.'

'Yes,' said Jesus. 'Treat him as your king.'

Jesus often told people what God's kingdom is like.

'God's kingdom's like a treasure hidden deeply underground. When you find it, you sell everything to buy it—and all the ground around.

'God's kingdom is like the most precious pearl on earth. You'd give your whole life for it. That is what it's worth.

'The more you give yourself to God, the more you know it's true; God's kingdom is not just in heaven; God's kingdom is in you!'

The churning turning lake

Mark 4:35–41

It wasn't stormy when they set out, but it was now! The wind churned and turned. The waves churned and turned. The boat churned and turned.

Jesus wasn't worried, not one little bit. He was sound asleep in the back of the boat. His friends were about to sink to the bottom of the lake! The boat tossed up and down.

'Wake up, Jesus,' they said. 'We're going to drown!'

Jesus stood and stretched out his hand.

'Keep calm,' he said to the churning turning wind.

'Keep calm,' he said to the churning turning waves.

'Keep calm,' he said to his churning turning friends. 'Why are you so afraid? Trust me and you can be brave.'

The storm stopped.

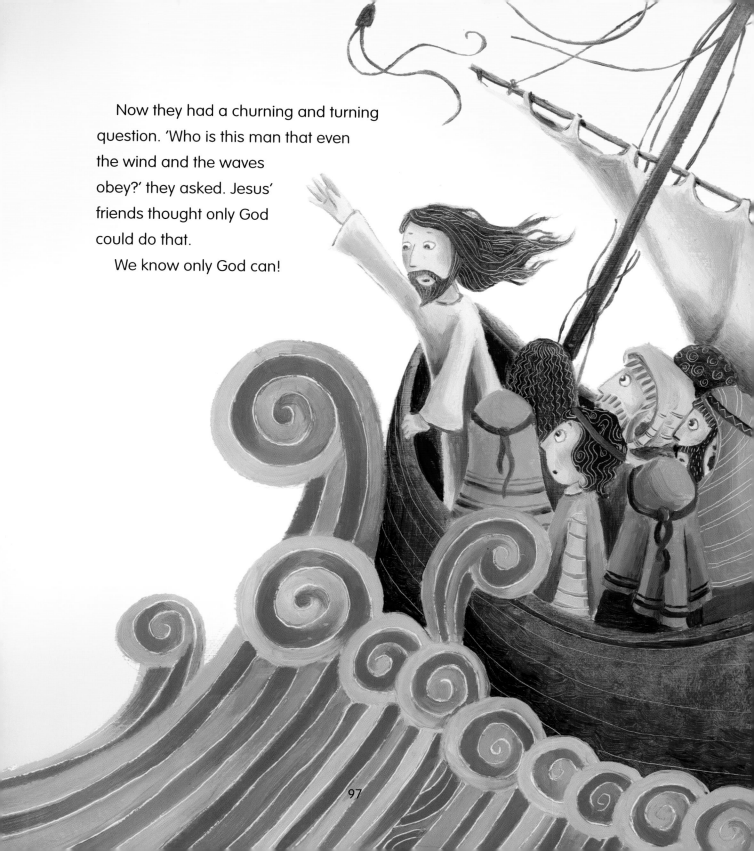

Now they had a churning and turning question. 'Who is this man that even the wind and the waves obey?' they asked. Jesus' friends thought only God could do that.

We know only God can!

97

A fabulous feast

Matthew 14:13–21; Mark 6:30–44; Luke 9:10–17; John 6:1–14

Thousands of people had been with Jesus and his friends all day.

'It's time to eat,' Jesus said to Philip. 'Where can we buy them some bread and meat?'

'Are you being funny?' said Philip. 'We don't have much money. And we'd never find enough food for everybody!'

But Jesus knew what he was going to do.

'Ask around the crowd,' he said to his friends.

A little boy stood beside Andrew.

'You can have my lunch,' he said.

'It's only two fish and five pieces of bread,' said Andrew.

'Is everyone sitting down?' Jesus smiled. 'Let's eat!'

Then Jesus thanked God for the food they all shared. There was plenty for everyone with more to spare.

Everyone was amazed by what Jesus had done.

The crowd began to whisper, 'He's the Promised One!'

When they followed him the next day, Jesus said, 'People need me to live. I am like bread.'

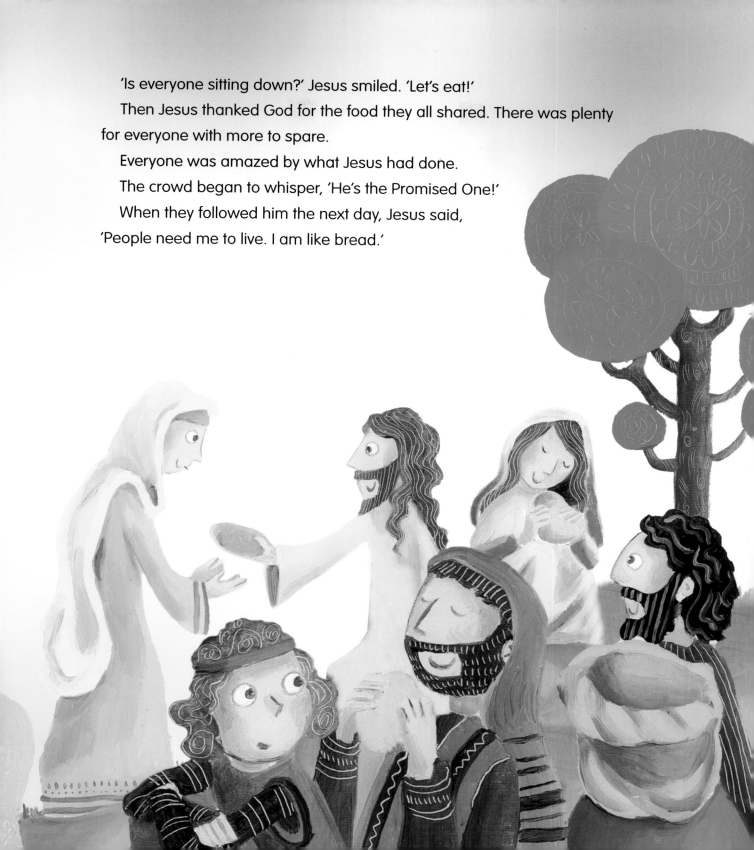

Waterwalkers

Matthew 14:22–33; Mark 6:45–52; John 6:16–21

The sea was rough. The rowing was tough. Jesus' friends were in trouble.
Suddenly, they saw something in the night. They were terrified.

'There's a g-g-ghost coming toward us!' they cried.

'Take courage,' said Jesus. 'It's me.'

'If it's really you,' said Peter, 'let me come to you.'

'Come on,' said Jesus. 'You can walk on water too!'

Peter stepped out on to the sea. He kept his eyes on Jesus. Everything was going well. But when he heard the wind, his fear swamped him. He looked down and began to drown.

'Save me, Lord!' he cried.

'Your faith is so small,' said Jesus. 'Why did you doubt?' He took Peter's hand and helped him out.

They got back into the boat. The wind stopped. The sea was still. They were safely on the shore. Everyone was amazed by what Jesus had done. They worshipped him and said, 'You are God's son!'

The good neighbour

Luke 10:25–37

A man was travelling on a lonely road. He walked up a hill. When he got to the top he stopped.

Suddenly some robbers hit him on the head, left him half dead and took everything he had.

A priest walked up the hill. When he got to the top he saw the man but didn't stop.

A temple helper walked up the hill. When he got to the top he didn't stop either!

A stranger from another country went up the hill on a donkey. But when he got to the top, clip clop, he stopped and hopped down.

'Poor man!' he said and bandaged his head.

He put the man on his donkey, and led the donkey down the hill. He took the man to an inn and cared for him. When he had to go away for a while, he paid the innkeeper to take care of the man.

Now Jesus had a question for the teacher.

'Who was the good neighbour and what did he do? You must be a good neighbour too.'

The busy sister and the big meal

Luke 10:38–42

Martha and Mary were happy when
Jesus and his friends came to visit. While
Martha got busy making a feast, Mary
sat and listened at Jesus' feet.

Martha scrubbed, peeled, diced and sliced. Mary didn't.
Martha measured, mixed, kneaded and baked. Mary didn't.
Martha set the table and poured the wine. Mary didn't.

'It's not fair,' Martha puffed. 'I'm doing all the work,' Martha whined. 'I've had enough!' Martha huffed. 'I'm being busy!' she said to Jesus. 'Mary is being lazy! Will you ask her to help?'

'Dear Martha, can't you see?' Jesus smiled. 'Mary is spending time with me. While you are busy being stressed, Mary has chosen what is best.'

We are blessed when we spend time with Jesus.

The good shepherd

Matthew 18:12–14; Luke 15:3–7; John 10:11–15

If a shepherd has a lot of sheep and one sheep leaps away, he leaves the lot safe on the spot for the one that got away. He will look here and there and everywhere. He will walk and climb and run. Day or night he will never stop until he finds that one. He brings the sheep home safe and sound and leaps for joy that his sheep is found.

'Heaven has a happy day,' said Jesus, 'when anyone chooses to live God's way.'

'I am the good shepherd,' Jesus said. 'I know all my sheep by name.

'No matter where they wander, I love them just the same. I will give my life to save them, no matter what the cost. If you want to follow me, you must love the people who are lost.'

God loves everyone—no matter what they're like.

Ten men well again

Luke 17:11–19

Ten men wanted to be well again. They saw Jesus passing by.

'Jesus, help us! Please!' they cried.

Their faces were covered with scars and their skin was covered with sores. They couldn't live with their families any more. Jesus looked, and felt their pain.

'Go and show the priest your skin,' said Jesus. 'You will all be well and can go home again.'

As the ten men began to go, their skin got better! They ran off happily. Only one man ran back to thank Jesus for healing his disease. He praised God and fell down on his knees.

'Thank you, Jesus,' he said.

'I made ten men well again,' said Jesus. 'I am glad you said thank you.'

Jesus is glad when we thank him too.

The power over death

John 11:1–44

When Lazarus died, Jesus cried. Even though he knew it would happen; even though he knew he could have stopped it. People were crying together because they missed Lazarus so much.

'Where were you?' sobbed Martha when she saw Jesus coming. 'My brother died! If you had been here to make him better, he would still be alive!'

'Everyone dies, Martha,' Jesus said softly. 'But it isn't the end. Everyone who believes in me will one day live again. Do you believe?'

'I believe you are the one that God promised to send,' said Martha.

Martha went to get Mary. Mary ran to Jesus. She fell at his feet and cried.

They took Jesus to the tomb where Lazarus was buried.

'Roll the stone away,' Jesus said.

Everyone was surprised.

'He's been dead for four days!' said Martha.

'I have power over death,' Jesus said.

Everyone held their breath.

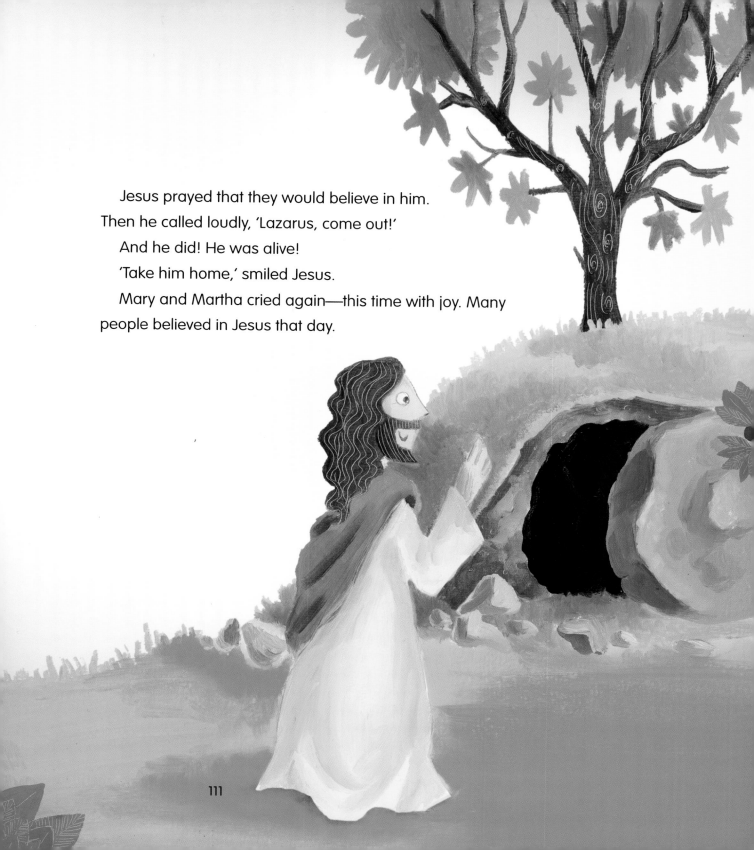

Jesus prayed that they would believe in him.
Then he called loudly, 'Lazarus, come out!'

And he did! He was alive!

'Take him home,' smiled Jesus.

Mary and Martha cried again—this time with joy. Many
people believed in Jesus that day.

111

The honest man's prayer

Luke 18:9–14

Jesus told this story to some people who thought they were better than others.

Two men went to the temple to pray. One man thought he was better than the other. He stood up proud and prayed out loud.

'Thank you, God. I am so good. I always do the things I should. I give my money. I keep the rules. I spend my time in prayer. I'm not like that man over there.'

The other man knew he wasn't always good. He didn't always do the things he should.

He hung his head and sadly said,
'Forgive me, God, for the things I've
done. I know that I'm the guilty one.'

Which prayer do you think God
answered?

'If you pray for show, God will
know,' Jesus said.

If you pray from your heart, God
will hear.

Jesus blesses the children

Matthew 19:13–15; Mark 10:13–16; Luke 18:15–17

Jesus was busy. People needed his help. They called out to him and crowded around him everywhere he went. They wanted Jesus to heal them with his touch. But some people who came to see him didn't need very much. Parents wanted Jesus to bless their children and pray. But his friends thought they were a bother and said, 'Go away!'

'Jesus has too much to do,' they said. 'He has no time to spend with you.'

When Jesus heard this he was cross.

'That's not true!' he said. 'Let the children come.'

He talked with them and blessed them and prayed for every single one.

'God's kingdom is full of children,' he said to his friends and smiled. 'If you want to get into God's kingdom, you must trust me like a child.'

Blind man sees

Mark 10:46–52

The coming crowd was very loud. Bartimaeus could hear them walking. He could hear them talking. But he couldn't see them. Bartimaeus was blind. He sat begging by the side of the road.

'What's going on?' he called out. 'Who is there?'

'Jesus is coming,' someone finally said.

Bartimaeus began to shout, 'Jesus! Help me!'

'Hush! Shush! Be quiet!' said the crowd.

But Bartimaeus didn't listen. He just shouted louder, 'Jesus! Over here! Help me!'

When Jesus heard, he stopped and turned. 'Tell him to come to me,' he said.

'Cheer up! Get up! Come on!' said the crowd. 'Jesus is calling you!'

Bartimaeus jumped to his feet and felt his way to Jesus.

'What do you want from me?' Jesus said tenderly.

'Teacher!' Bartimaeus said. 'I want to see!'

'Go!' said Jesus, smiling. 'Your faith has given you sight. Open your eyes!'

Suddenly Bartimaeus could see everything. He could see everyone. And Bartimaeus could see Jesus!

'I can see! I can see! I can see!' he shouted happily.

'He can see! He can see! He can see!' the crowd cheered.

Bartimaeus joined the crowd along the road,

but it was really Jesus he followed.

117

The little man and the big change

Luke 19:1–10

Lots of people crowded around Jesus. Everyone wanted to see him and hear what he said.

Zacchaeus wanted to see him too. But, no matter how hard he tried, he couldn't see over and he couldn't see through. He was just too small.

'I can't see Jesus at all,' said Zacchaeus. 'But I can see a tree.' So he climbed up to get a good view. Jesus got a good view too.

'Come down, Zacchaeus,' Jesus said. 'I'd like to spend some time with you! Let's go to your house.'

It turns out that Jesus knew more about Zacchaeus than just his name. Zacchaeus had his own kind of fame. He was rich because he took money that didn't belong to him.

'He's a cheat!' said the people to each other.

'I want to change!' said Zacchaeus to Jesus. 'I will give half of all I have to those who need it. And if I've cheated anyone, I will pay them back—and four times more!'

'Zacchaeus! You have been saved today!' Jesus said. 'I came to help people to live God's way.'

Here comes the King

Matthew 21:1–11; Mark 11:1–10; Luke 19:37–40; John 12:12–19

Jesus and his friends were walking to Jerusalem. When they were almost there, Jesus said, 'There is a donkey in the next town. No one has ever ridden it. Find it and bring it here.'

Now the donkey didn't buck when Jesus sat on his back. It didn't kick or bray, not even when the crowd scattered their coats along the way.

People waved palm branches in the air. There was so much celebration! Almost everyone began to cheer!

'The king is coming! King Jesus is here!'

Some people were not so happy. They didn't like what Jesus did or said. They were angry. They didn't believe that Jesus was the one God sent.

'Stop them cheering!' they said to Jesus. 'What's this nonsense all about?'

'I could keep them quiet,' Jesus smiled, 'but the stones would still cry out!'

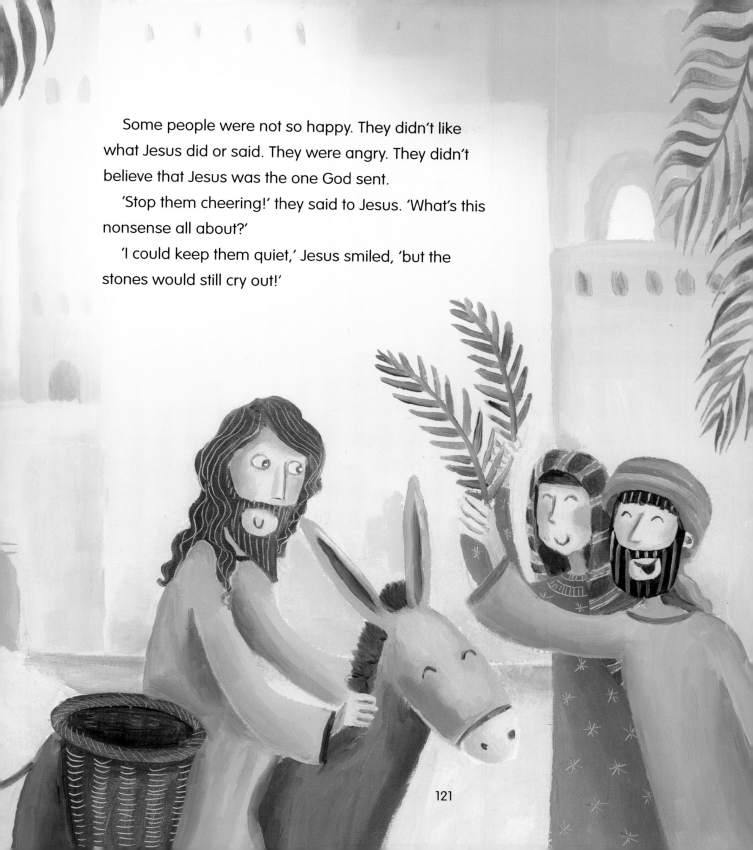

Dusty dirty feet

John 13:1–20

It had been a dusty day. It would soon be time to eat. Jesus and his friends had very dirty feet. Jesus filled a bowl with water and began to wash each one. Then he dried them with a towel as a servant would have done.

'I can't let you wash my feet, Lord!' Peter said. 'That's not your job to do!'

'Everyone is a servant in my kingdom,' said Jesus. 'If you want to be part of it, you must let me serve you too.'

'Don't just wash my feet, then!' said Peter. 'Wash my hands and my head!'

'Oh Peter, the rest of you is clean!' Jesus said. 'I just need to wash your feet, my friend.'

Then Jesus asked them all, 'Do you understand what I have done for you? Show your love by serving others as I have served you.'

The special supper

Matthew 26:17–29; Mark 14:12–25; Luke 22:7–23; John 13:18–30

Jesus was eating with his friends. But he was thinking about his enemies.

'Some people hate me,' Jesus said. 'They don't believe God sent me. They are going to kill me.'

'We won't let that happen!' said Jesus' friends.

'It already is,' said Jesus. 'One of you has even promised to help them find me.'

124

They were shocked. They wondered who it might be. Judas slipped out of the door quietly.

Jesus took some bread and broke it. He thanked God and gave it to them.

'This is what is going to happen to my body,' he said. 'It will be broken for you.'

Then he poured some red wine. He thanked God for it and gave it to them.

'This is what is going to happen to my blood,' he said. 'It will be poured out for you.

'I am going to die, just as it was written, so that people can be forgiven. But I am also going to live again and go home to God in heaven. One day, you will come too. Every time you eat and drink, this is what to do,' said Jesus. 'Remember that I love you and have given my life for you.'

In the garden

Matthew 26:31–56; Mark 14:27–50; Luke 22:39–53; John 18:1–11

It was dark outside. Jesus felt dark inside. He needed help to be brave. He asked his friends to go into the garden with him and pray.

Jesus told them, 'You will all deny me or desert me before the night is through.'

'Not me!' said Peter. 'It can't be true!'

'Yes,' said Jesus, 'even you. The rooster will crow twice at dawn. You will say that you don't know me three times by then.'

'I will never deny your name!' said Peter. 'I would die first!' And all the others said the same.

Jesus' friends fell asleep. Jesus prayed all night long.

'I am your son,' he said to his Father God. 'I will do what must be done!'

Light flooded the garden. A crowd came with torches, swords and clubs. Judas came with a kiss.

'Friend,' said Jesus. 'Are you betraying me like this?'

Most of Jesus' friends ran away. But Peter pulled out a sword.

'Put it down,' said Jesus calmly. 'Angels could save me if I called. But who would save you then? I am the Lord.'

Peter denies Jesus

Matthew 26:69–75; Mark 14:66–72; Luke 22:54–62; John 18:15–18, 25–27

Peter was afraid but he followed just the same. He wanted to know what would happen. He wanted to be close to his friend. While soldiers took Jesus inside a house, Peter stood outside, warming himself by a fire. A servant was looking at him.

'You were with Jesus!' she said.

Peter looked surprised.

'Who, me?' he answered. 'No!'

Just then, a rooster began to crow.

A little while later another servant said, 'I'm sure you are one of his friends.'

'I don't even know him!' Peter lied.

'You talk just like them,' someone else replied.

'I tell you,' Peter swore, 'I do not know the man!'

And even as he said it, the rooster crowed again.

Peter knew he had broken his promise to be true. He was so sorry he felt his heart was breaking too.

Just then, the guards took Jesus by. Jesus turned to Peter and looked him in the eye. Peter felt so ashamed that he cried.

Jesus dies on a cross

Matthew 27:1–50; Mark 15:1–37; Luke 23:1–46; John 19:1–30

Jesus did not hate those who hated him. He did not hate those who told lies about him. He did not hate those who ordered him to die. He did not hate those who beat him until he bled or pushed a thorny crown on to his head. He did not hate the soldiers who led him to the place where he would be killed. He did not hate them when they nailed him to a cross.

He did not hate the people who stood there on the hill.

'If you are the one God sent, come down from the cross,' they jeered. 'You can't even save yourself. How can you save us?'

Jesus did not hate his enemies. He loved them instead.

'Father, forgive them,' he said.

Many who loved Jesus were also there. They watched and wept and waited. It took long hours for Jesus to die. The sky went dark.

'My God, my God,' Jesus cried, 'why have you left me all alone?'

When the time had come Jesus whispered, 'It is done!'

Then Jesus died for everyone.

The empty tomb

John 20:1–18

Mary was sad. She walked to Jesus' tomb in the dim light of dawn. But the stone was rolled away! The tomb was empty! Jesus was gone! She ran straight away to tell Peter and John.

'Someone has taken Jesus' body!' she cried.

Peter and John couldn't believe it. They ran to the tomb, side by side. The only thing they found were the grave clothes Jesus had been buried in.

Mary stood crying all alone when they had gone. When she looked into the tomb again, there were two angels where Jesus' body should have been.

'Why are you crying?' the angels asked.

'I can't find Jesus!' Mary said through her tears.

Then she thought she saw the gardener standing near.

'Did you take Jesus?' she asked him. 'Please tell me where!'

'Mary,' said the man.

Mary stopped and stared, for she knew him then. It was Jesus! Jesus was alive again!

'Go and tell the others that I am alive,' Jesus said.

Mary could hardly believe it! It was such a surprise! She ran and told Jesus' friends, 'Jesus is alive—and I have seen him with my own eyes!'

Thomas believes

Luke 24:36–49; John 20:19–29

Jesus' friends were afraid. They met behind locked doors. Suddenly Jesus appeared and said, 'Peace be yours.'

They thought he was a ghost!

Jesus showed them his hands, his feet, his side. Then they ate together.

'It's true! It's you!' they cried.

'Just as the Father sent me,' he said, 'I am sending you. The Holy Spirit will come. He will help you do what I would do.'

Now Thomas wasn't there when Jesus appeared.

'Thomas!' they said. 'We have seen the Lord!'

'I will not believe,' said Thomas, 'unless I touch his wounds for myself.'

A week later, Jesus' friends were together as before. Suddenly Jesus was there again and said, 'Peace be yours.'

Then he said to Thomas, 'Touch my hands and side. Have faith and believe— be satisfied.'

Thomas didn't need to touch him!

'My Lord and God,' was all that he could say.

'You believe in me because you have seen me,' said Jesus. 'Happy are those who have never seen but believe in me anyway.'

Do you love me?

John 21:1–16

It was morning. Peter and some of Jesus' friends had been fishing all night, and not got a nibble. The last time this happened, Jesus filled their nets and Peter left everything to follow him. Now Peter didn't know what to do. He had denied even knowing Jesus. He felt disappointed in himself and thought Jesus would feel the same.

Suddenly, a man on the shore gave a shout. 'Catch anything?'

'Not a nibble,' Peter shouted back.

'Try again, friend!' the man said.

Something felt familiar. Peter and his friends put their net back in. Suddenly, it was full of fish. The feeling grew. John said, 'It's Jesus!' Suddenly, Peter knew too!

'Jesus! It's Jesus!' he shouted as he jumped in and swam to shore!

Jesus was cooking breakfast on the beach.

'Where's the fish?' he smiled at Peter.

Soon Peter helped the others drag the net to land. Everyone was so happy. It was the best breakfast ever.

'Peter, do you love me?' asked Jesus.

'Oh, you know I do!' said Peter.

'Then take care of my friends, and love them as I have loved you.'

Home to heaven

Matthew 28:16–20; Mark 16:15–20; Luke 24:44–53; Acts 1:6–11

Jesus met with his friends often. They spent time walking and talking and eating together. They were happy that Jesus was alive! They felt brave having him near. But now it was time for Jesus to go home to heaven. They met together one last time.

'God has given me power over earth and heaven,' Jesus said. 'It's your job to tell everyone everywhere the good news. Everyone can be my friend. All can be forgiven.

'Teach people to believe in me and to live God's way. Whenever you worry or wonder, remember I'm with you always.

'You must wait now in Jerusalem. The Holy Spirit will come. He will give you all the power you need to do what must be done.'

Then Jesus went into heaven. He was surrounded by clouds. His friends couldn't stop looking at where he disappeared. They didn't know what to do or say!

Then two angels appeared. 'Why are you standing here looking sad?' they asked. 'He'll be back again some day.'

The Holy Spirit comes to help

Acts 2:1–47

Jesus' friends were in Jerusalem. They were waiting and praying for the Holy Spirit to come. Suddenly, there was a sound like a rushing wind. Then something like a small flame of fire settled on each one. They knew the Holy Spirit had filled them. They began to speak in languages they'd never heard before!

Jerusalem was filled with visitors from all over the world. They were astonished by what they heard. Jesus' friends were speaking and they could understand every word!

'How can this be?' said many. 'This is very odd! They are speaking to me in my own language about the love of God!'

'They are out of their minds,' said others. 'They must be drunk on wine!'

But Peter was bold and told them about all that Jesus had done.

'We can all be forgiven for the things we do wrong. God sent Jesus to save us. God loves everyone!'

Thousands of people believed in Jesus and were baptised that day!

They met to worship God, to share their belongings and to pray. They asked the Holy Spirit to help them live God's way.